DEMOCRACY REVIVAL

MASTERING THE BEST WAYS TO RESCUE AMERICA THROUGH EASY MEANS

SUNNY CHRIS

ISBN : 9798329938890
written by: Sunny Chris
year of publication: 2024

THIS BOOK BELONGS TO:

____

____

____

Table of Content

Democracy Revival: Mastering the Best Ways to Rescue America Through Easy Means

1. Introduction: The Call for Renewal
   - Understanding the Challenges
   - The Importance of Citizen Engagement

Introduction: The Call for Renewal
Understanding the Challenges

The United States has seen significant changes in the last few decades that have tested the country's democratic foundations. The political environment has turned into a war zone, characterized by extreme division, pervasive disinformation, and rising institutional mistrust. The public's confidence in democracy has been undermined by these difficulties, which have also brought to light weaknesses that, if ignored, could jeopardize the fundamental ideas upon which the country was founded.

Of these difficulties, political polarization is arguably the most evident and widespread. The days of bipartisan cooperation are long gone; in their place, political views are becoming increasingly divisive. Media outlets and social media platforms that foster echo chambers, strengthening preexisting opinions and escalating antagonism toward opposing viewpoints, frequently aggravate this divide. In such a setting, it is almost impossible to have a productive conversation because people withdraw into their ideological corners and see compromise as a betrayal rather than as a must for advancement.

In this divisive environment, disinformation has become a powerful tool. Although the internet is an effective medium for disseminating information, it has also turned into a haven for conspiracy theories and incorrect information. Like wildfire, fake news spreads quickly, frequently surpassing the truth and leaving a path of distrust and uncertainty in its wake. Because of this tendency, it is harder for the general population to distinguish between fact and fiction, which impairs their ability to make educated decisions.

Uncertainty about democratic institutions is still another major obstacle. Many people now doubt the legitimacy and efficacy of government institutions due to scandals, alleged corruption, and inefficiencies. Apathy and disengagement ensue when people lose trust in the institutions created to uphold their rights and in their leaders. This disengagement is especially worrying since it erodes civic obligation and voting turnout, which further undermines the democratic process.

Disenfranchisement among excluded people is exacerbated by systemic injustices and economic imbalances. People become less motivated to engage in the democratic process when they believe that the odds are stacked against them, that their opinions are unimportant, and that they do not have access to the same possibilities as others. To make sure that democracy benefits everyone, not just the wealthy and powerful, these fundamental problems need to be resolved.

The Value of Involvement by Citizens

In spite of these formidable obstacles, there is a strong prospect for renewal —a chance to revitalize democracy by encouraging citizens to take an active role in it. Democracy is participation at its core, and we can solve the structural problems endangering our democratic ideals by working together. The goal of this book, "Democracy Revival: Mastering the Best Ways to Rescue America Through Easy Means," is to offer readers a road map for this revitalization by outlining doable tactics for becoming change agents.

A thriving democracy is built on the foundation of citizen engagement. Individuals may effect significant change in society at all levels when they are knowledgeable, engaged, and empowered. Education is the first step in this connection. Comprehending democratic ideas, procedures, and establishments endows citizens with the erudition necessary to maneuver through and impact the political terrain. By reassuring people that their opinions count and that they have the ability to influence both their communities and the country, civic education promotes a sense of action and responsibility.

Despite the fact that voting is an essential civic duty, the US nonetheless has a dismal voter turnout rate. Many eligible voters abstain from voting, frequently claiming a sense of disenfranchised or doubts about the significance of their vote. Voting is emphasized in this text as a crucial instrument for accountability and change. Voting in elections gives voters the power to shape public policy, select leaders who share their ideals, and hold those officials responsible for their deeds.

In addition to voting, local groups and grassroots movements are essential for promoting civic engagement. These organizations give people a place to gather, exchange ideas, and collaborate on projects. Significant social and political change has historically been fueled by grassroots activity, as seen in the environmental movement and the civil rights movement. Participating in these movements strengthens the voices of the individual and shows the group impact of coordinated, neighborhood-based action.

Another essential component of civic participation is effective communication. In an age of divisiveness and disinformation, it is crucial to promote civil, knowledgeable discourse. This book encourages readers to look for common ground and approach discussions with empathy and an open mind as it examines methods for mending rifts and having polite conversations. We can restore confidence and foster a more welcoming political atmosphere by placing a higher priority on constructive communication.

An Appeal for Intervention

All citizens are urged to take action by the call for regeneration. It is a call to action to rise above passivity and disengagement, to see the value of group effort, and to assume accountability for our democracy's future. Our difficulties are great, but they are not insurmountable. By means of empowerment, engagement, and education, we may surmount the obstacles that impede democratic participation and construct a more robust and inclusive democratic system.

This book offers doable tactics and insightful perspectives on how people may support democracy's comeback. It provides a thorough manual on how to learn the most effective strategies to save America through approachable methods, enabling everyone to participate in civic life. Every chapter aims to provide readers with the necessary skills to effect change, ranging from comprehending the existing condition of democracy to empowering individuals and fostering communal ties.

To sum up, the cry for renewal is a cry to acknowledge both our own accountability and our group's strength. It serves as a reminder that democracy is an ongoing endeavor in which every person must actively participate. We can make sure that our democracy endures, our institutions are robust, and our country prospers by answering this call. Together, let's go out on this adventure, dedicated to bringing democracy back to life and ensuring that everyone has a better future.

NOW YOU CAN JOTT DOWN YOUR EXPECTATIONS FROM THIS BOOK ON THE NEXT PAGE

NOTE

Chapter 1: The State of Democracy
 - Current Challenges
 - Erosion of Trust in Institutions

Chapter 1: The State of Democracy
Understanding Current Challenges

American democracy is confronted with a number of issues in the modern world that jeopardize its core values. Political polarization has split society into ideological factions and fostered a "us versus them" mentality. This has been exacerbated by a more polarized media landscape. In addition to stifling fruitful discussion, this polarization impedes bipartisan cooperation, which makes it challenging for elected leaders to efficiently handle urgent situations.

The growth of digital echo chambers and disinformation deepen these divides even more. Conspiracy theories and extremist viewpoints are frequently amplified on social media platforms, which are meant to engage users through personalized content. This phenomena erodes public confidence in traditional news sources and feeds a vicious cycle of cynicism and mistrust towards established institutions by making it harder for the public to distinguish fact from fiction.

The Decline of Institutional Trust

There is a record lack of trust in democratic institutions. Citizens are generally disillusioned with government as a result of scandals, apparent corruption, and inefficiencies. Many believe that the political system solely serves special interests, that their opinions are not heard, and that public servants put their own interests before of the good of the public. Voter apathy, decreased participation rates, and a general feeling of alienation from the political process are all symptoms of this breakdown of confidence.

The judiciary is increasingly perceived via a partisan prism, despite having long been recognized as an unbiased arbiter of justice. Ideological differences are frequently reflected in decisions made on controversial matters, which adds to the public's mistrust of the justice system's impartiality and justice. The rule of law, which is essential to democracy, is at danger because of this alleged lack of impartiality.

Economic Inequalities and Disparities

Systemic injustices and economic inequality pose serious obstacles to democratic participation. Economic power is translated into political influence in an environment where the wealth gap between the rich and the poor is growing. In addition to undermining the idea of fair representation, this imbalance makes excluded people feel more alienated and resentful.

Disparities in work, healthcare, and education are examples of systemic problems that feed the cycle of disenfranchisement. People become less inclined to engage in the democratic process when they believe that the system is biased against them. In order to restore democracy and guarantee that every citizen has an equal say in determining the destiny of the country, it is imperative that these disparities be addressed.

Civic Education's Function

The battle against the problems confronting democracy depends heavily on civic education. A well-informed voter enables citizens to hold leaders accountable and makes smart decisions, which is crucial for a democracy to function. Sadly, many educational institutions have made civic education a low priority, leaving students ill-prepared to comprehend and participate in democratic processes.

In addition to teaching students about the workings of government, revitalizing civic education include encouraging media literacy, critical thinking, and an understanding of differing viewpoints. We can mitigate the impact of false information and divisiveness by providing citizens with the means to evaluate data and participate in productive discourse.

Grassroots Movements' Power

Notwithstanding these obstacles, grassroots movements provide a glimmer of hope for democracy's resurgence. In the past, grassroots action has been crucial in bringing about significant change, as seen by the civil rights movement and more current environmental and social justice campaigns. By utilizing the strength of group effort, these movements enable people to support laws that are in line with the interests and ideals of their local communities.

In order to mobilize people, raise awareness of important issues, and encourage a sense of community involvement, grassroots organizations are essential. Individuals can strengthen their voices and support a larger initiative to address systemic issues by joining these movements. Activists at the grassroots level show that common people may affect political decisions and the course of the nation.

Restoring Conversation and Overcoming Divides

It is essential to heal divisions and reestablish productive communication in order to confront the status of democracy today. This entails creating a setting where a range of viewpoints are respected and arguments are handled with decency and sensitivity. Even in the midst of enduring disagreements, decent discourse necessitates listening, comprehending, and finding common ground.

Addressing the root causes of division is another requirement for reestablishing discourse. This entails advancing media literacy, fostering candid dialogues, and endorsing venues that foster civil discourse. We can build a more inclusive political environment that represents the complexity of the American voter by placing a higher priority on discourse.

In conclusion, a way forward

America's democracy is at a critical juncture. The difficulties are great, but they also offer a chance for rebirth. We can create the foundation for a more robust and inclusive democracy by tackling polarization, dispelling false information, restoring faith in institutions, and encouraging civic engagement.

This chapter is a call to action, imploring readers to acknowledge their part in influencing democracy. Each of us has the ability to restore democracy, and by working together, we can get past the challenges facing our democratic principles. Let us pledge to create a future in which every citizen has the ability to make a difference and their voice is heard as we set out on this path toward the rebirth of democracy.

NOTE

Chapter 2: Empowering the Individual
   - Civic Education and Awareness
   - The Power of the Vote

Chapter 2: Empowering the Individual
Unlocking the Potential of Civic Education

In a democracy, education, more especially civic education, is the first step toward empowering people. This fundamental pillar provides individuals with the information, abilities, and comprehension needed to successfully negotiate the intricacies of governance, engage in civic life, and preserve democratic values.

The Value of Community Education

Civic education aims to develop critical thinking, civic duty, and a feeling of civic identity in addition to teaching political institutions and dates. It gives people the ability to understand how government works, recognize the value of active involvement, and assess elected officials' actions critically. Civic education is a crucial countermeasure in a time when partisan divides widen and misinformation proliferates unchecked, giving people the knowledge and skills to separate reality from fiction and make wise judgments.

Reforming Education and Empowering Students

In school curricula, civic education frequently receives insufficient emphasis despite its crucial role. A concentrated effort to incorporate comprehensive civic education programs into schools across the country is needed to close this gap. Schools can develop a new generation of engaged citizens who are aware of their rights and understand the responsibilities that come with citizenship by emphasizing civic literacy. Encouraging a participatory democracy in which each person feels empowered to make a significant contribution to the political process requires this educational transformation.

The Vote's Power: Democracy at Work

Voting is a fundamental component of individual empowerment in a democratic society. Voting is an essential tool for expressing political views, influencing policy decisions, and holding elected people responsible. It is not only a privilege. Nonetheless, American voter turnout frequently falls short of potential, especially in years when there isn't a presidential election and among disenfranchised communities.

Encouraging Voter Participation

It is necessary to remove obstacles like difficult voter registration processes, restrictive voting rules, and disillusioned indifference in order to promote voter participation. In order to promote more inclusion and guarantee that all views are heard in the democratic process, it is imperative that efforts be made to increase access to the voting booth, including through early voting, mail-in choices, and voter registration drives.

Voter Education and Activation

Campaigns for education are essential to increasing voter turnout and civic engagement. Organizations and local authorities can enable citizens to make informed decisions by teaching them about the importance of voting and how election results will affect their lives. Digital campaigns, door-to-door outreach programs, and grassroots campaigns are powerful instruments for energizing voters and creating a wave of support for important topics that appeal to a wide range of voters.

Creating Community Links: The Power of Group Initiative

Community is another environment in which empowerment flourishes. People can work together, promote common interests, and bring about change at the local level on platforms provided by civic groups, local organizations, and grassroots movements. These ties to the community help people feel like they belong and are strong, which gives them the confidence to take on local problems and have an impact on larger policy discussions.

Community-Based Initiatives: Their Significance

Initiatives rooted in the community play a critical role in directing personal empowerment toward group action. These initiatives—which range from planning neighborhood clean-ups to tackling socioeconomic disparities and promoting legislative reforms—showcase the transformative power of community engagement. Through resource mobilization, collaboration, and amplification of marginalized voices, local groups enable individuals to take an active role in determining the course of their communities.

Boosting Interpersonal Harmony

Community ties foster a sense of civic duty and pride in addition to enhancing social cohesiveness. Communities become stronger in the face of adversity and better equipped to handle complicated problems when they cultivate relationships based on mutual respect, trust, and shared ideals. Building consensus, mending divisions, and achieving group objectives that benefit society as a whole all depend on this unity.

Using Technology: Digital Instruments for Participation in Democracy

In the era of digitalization, technology has a growing impact on people's ability to participate in democracy. There are new channels for civic involvement, mobilization, and communication thanks to social media platforms, online discussion boards, and digital advocacy tools. With the aid of these internet technologies, people can coordinate campaigns that cross national lines, instantly share information, and connect with other activists who share their values.

Using Digital Platforms to Their Full Potential

Digital platforms magnify individual voices globally and democratize access to knowledge. They hold elected leaders responsible to their constituents, encourage open communication, and enable dialogue. Digital tools also enable people to sign petitions, take part in virtual town halls, and participate in real-time policy discussions, turning them from passive spectators into active participants in democratic decision-making.

Managing Difficulties in the Digital Age

Nevertheless, there are drawbacks to using digital technologies in democracies, such as the propagation of false information, privacy issues, and algorithmic biases that exacerbate echo chambers. Promoting media literacy, arguing for moral digital behavior, and protecting democratic processes from malevolent intervention are necessary to meet these issues. People may fully utilize technology to bolster democracy and increase their influence by encouraging inclusive online communities and responsible digital citizenship.

In conclusion, Developing Today's Leaders of Tomorrow

The transforming force of individual empowerment in a democratic society is emphasized in Chapter 2. Through ethical use of digital tools, voter engagement, civic education, and community connections, people can become change agents both within and outside of their communities. This chapter is a call to action, imploring readers to seize the chance for meaningful civic engagement and to acknowledge their own potential as agents of democratic transformation. Individuals can contribute to the development of a more responsive, inclusive, and resilient democracy that represents the many views and goals of all Americans by learning how to effectively empower themselves and others using easily accessible tools.

Let us honor democracy's core principles of equality, fairness, and accountability as we set out on this empowerment journey. Together, we can create a future in which every person has the chance to prosper and make a positive contribution to society. By working together, we can preserve and strengthen America's democratic promise so that future generations can continue to enjoy it.

NOTE

Chapter 3: Building Community Connections
  - Grassroots Movements
  - The Role of Local Organizations

Chapter 3: Building Community Connections
The Power of Grassroots Movements

Reviving democracy is really about creating ties inside the community. Against a backdrop of societal disintegration and political divisiveness, grassroots movements become potent agents of change. These movements use the combined strength of people who are motivated by similar goals, values, and concerns to take on urgent political, social, and economic issues.

The Beginnings and Significance of Citizen Movements

Throughout history, social justice reforms, environmental preservation, and civil rights have all benefited greatly from the efforts of grassroots movements. From the Martin Luther King Jr.-led civil rights movement to more recent movements calling for racial fairness and action against climate change, grassroots activism has changed public discourse, impacted governmental agendas, and inspired communities to demand systemic change.

The Power of Group Initiative
Fundamentally, grassroots movements are prime examples of the power of group effort. Through the coordination of demonstrations, marches, rallies, and advocacy campaigns, they enable regular people to become change agents. Individuals strengthen their voices, bring important concerns to the public's attention, and rally support for legislative changes that align with community values through these coordinated activities.

Boosting Regional Voices

Focusing on local empowerment and engagement is one of the hallmarks of grassroots movements. Grassroots groups make sure that underprivileged communities' needs are met and that underrepresented voices are heard by promoting inclusive decision-making processes and giving priority to community-driven solutions. In addition to enhancing social cohesiveness, this localized strategy increases resistance to outside forces and structural injustices.

Local Organizations' Role

Local groups and civic associations, which function as essential centers of social contact and civic participation, are essential to creating a sense of community. These groups serve a variety of roles in promoting community cohesion and addressing local issues; they include nonprofits, faith-based organizations, neighborhood associations, and community centers.

Initiatives Based in the Community

Community-based projects that foster civic engagement, social cohesiveness, and cooperative problem-solving are led by local organizations. Whether planning volunteer endeavors, arranging cultural gatherings, or offering social services, these programs foster a sense of community and solidarity among locals. Additionally, they give locals a chance to work together, pool resources, and promote laws that improve the welfare of the community.

Increasing Social Capital

The idea of social capital emphasizes the role that neighborhood associations play in fostering ties within the community. Social capital is defined as the networks of relationships, reciprocity standards, and shared trust within a community. Local groups provide social capital and enable communities to confront common issues including public health issues, educational discrepancies, and economic disparities by encouraging trust and cooperation amongst a variety of stakeholders.

Promoting Local Solutions

Local groups support regional approaches to regional problems. They organize support for neighborhood-driven projects, involve locals in grassroots advocacy campaigns, and petition elected authorities for changes to policies. These groups make sure that community objectives shape public policies and investments that reflect the needs and ambitions of citizens by elevating local voices and encouraging participatory decision-making.

Digital Engagement and Local Movements

Grassroots movements use social media and technology in the digital age to spread their message and get more attention. Using digital tools, organizers can instantly communicate information, rally supporters, and plan virtual events that take place anywhere in the world. Digital storytelling, online petitions, and social media campaigns enable people to participate in activism at any time and from any location, promoting a sense of interconnectedness and group unity across borders.

Using the Internet for Advocacy

Digital advocacy platforms enable people to engage in political discourse and civic involvement while also democratizing access to information. Grassroots movements may impact public opinion and policy results, rally followers, and magnify their messages by utilizing the power of internet advocacy. Activists may create momentum, increase awareness, and effect significant change at the local and national levels by utilizing data-driven strategies, digital storytelling approaches, and online organizing tools.

Handling Difficulties

But there are drawbacks to the digital world as well, such as false information spreading, privacy issues, and algorithmic biases that influence how people interact online. Media literacy, the moral use of data, and a dedication to advancing inclusive online communities that encourage civil discourse and civic involvement are necessary for effective digital activism. Through overcoming these obstacles, grassroots movements will be able to fully utilize digital platforms to further democratic ideals, social justice, and community empowerment in the creation of a more just and equitable society.

In summary, bolstering democracy from the foundation up

The importance of fostering neighborhood ties and grassroots movements in reviving democracy is emphasized in Chapter 3. Through the promotion of civic involvement, the cultivation of inclusive decision-making, and the responsible use of digital resources, individuals and local organizations may effectively strengthen communities, champion fair policies, and elevate the perspectives of underrepresented populations. This chapter is a call to action, imploring readers to acknowledge the role that grassroots activity, online advocacy, and community solidarity will play in determining the course of democracy in the future.

Let's collaborate to build democracy from the ground up as we embrace the ideas of empowerment and group action. A more inclusive, responsive, and resilient democracy—one that represents the many voices and ambitions of all Americans—can be achieved by individuals by learning the most effective strategies for creating community connections using easily available tools. By working together, we can preserve and strengthen America's democratic promise so that future generations can continue to enjoy it.

NOTE

Chapter 4: Effective Communication in Politics
 - Bridging Divides
 - Engaging in Civil Discourse

Chapter 4: Effective Communication in Politics Bridging Divides: Fostering Unity in Diversity

Good communication is essential to a functioning democracy. In a time of increasing social and political division, it is crucial to build bridges across opposing viewpoints in order to advance understanding, encourage harmony, and accomplish shared objectives. This chapter examines how democratic institutions may be strengthened, inclusive discourse can be fostered, and ideological divides can be closed through effective communication.

Comprehending Political Polarization

Political polarization is the term used to describe how different people's and groups' political beliefs and attitudes diverge. It fosters a "us versus them" mentality in which disagreements are magnified and agreement is difficult to come by. Echo chambers in the media and online, where people are largely exposed to information that confirms their preexisting opinions, enhance this polarization and deepen divisions.

The Importance of Clear Communication

Good communication encourages discussion, empathy, and understanding between parties, which makes it an effective tool for mending rifts. It entails politely conversing, actively listening to others who hold different opinions, and looking for areas of agreement. Communicators can foster an inclusive political discourse by bridging ideological gaps and addressing concerns with empathy and acknowledging a range of opinions.

Encouraging Talk That Is Inclusive

Creating forums where people from different backgrounds feel at ease sharing their opinions and taking part in conversations is a key component of inclusive communication. It entails establishing guidelines for civil discourse, appreciating the diversity of viewpoints, and creating a space where everyone may be heard. By encouraging empathy and respect for one another, inclusive discourse not only improves the standard of decision-making but also fortifies societal cohesiveness.

Having Civil Conversations: Constructive Dialogue's Foundation

The cornerstone of democratic participation is civil discourse, which includes polite conversation, reasoned argumentation, and the sharing of views without animosity or personal assault. It inspires people to have thoughtful conversations, question presumptions, and look for common ground on divisive topics. The concepts of polite conversation are examined in this part, along with tactics for encouraging fruitful conversation in political settings.

Civil Discourse Principles

Participants in civil debate must conduct themselves in a respectful, polite manner and be receptive to opposing points of view. It entails paying close attention when others are speaking, accepting the legitimacy of different viewpoints, and abstaining from insulting or provocative words. By emphasizing concepts over specific people, polite conversation creates a space where people can discuss difficult topics, confront presumptions, and come to well-informed conclusions.

Techniques for Encouraging Positive Communication

Fostering positive communication requires developing abilities like empathy, critical thinking, and active listening. It calls for establishing ground rules for polite conversation, deciding on shared discussion objectives, and providing chances for group problem-solving. Communicators can create consensus on policy solutions that benefit society as a whole and overcome ideological gaps by highlighting shared values and mutual interests.

Making the Most of Communication and Media Channels

Using the media and communication channels to reach a variety of audiences, clearly communicate messages, and provoke thought-provoking discussion among stakeholders is another aspect of effective political communication. Politicians, advocacy groups, and civic organizations can use digital technologies, social media platforms, and traditional media channels to spread information, rally support, and sway public opinion.

Overcoming Obstacles in Media Communication

Effective political communication is hampered by the spread of false information, partisan media bias, and algorithmic filtering. Promoting media literacy, fact-checking information, and making media companies responsible for ethical reporting practices are necessary to address these issues. Communicators can increase the credibility of their communications and develop public trust by promoting transparency and honesty in media messaging.

Political Leadership's Function

Setting the tone for productive dialogue and encouraging polite conversation is a critical responsibility of political leaders. Through the demonstration of courteous conduct, the promotion of bipartisan cooperation, and the emphasis on inclusive discourse, leaders have the ability to inspire confidence, reconcile ideological differences, and develop a collaborative culture inside governmental institutions. Effective communication leadership entails stating a clear vision, involving stakeholders in the decision-making process, and promoting policies that take into account the varied interests of stakeholders.

In summary, Promoting Democracy via Efficient Communication

The transformative impact of excellent communication in reviving democracy and enhancing civic engagement is highlighted in Chapter 4. Building consensus, addressing systemic issues, and advancing common goals for the good of society can all be accomplished by people and groups through bridging ideological gaps, encouraging inclusive dialogue, and growing civil discourse. This chapter is a call to action, imploring readers to embrace chances for deep conversation and cooperation as well as to acknowledge the significance of communication abilities in political participation.

Let us maintain the values of transparency, empathy, and respect in our communications while we work through the challenges of contemporary democracy. People may help create a more responsive, inclusive, and resilient democracy that values diversity and fosters unity among people by learning the best ways to communicate effectively using accessible channels. By working together, we can use communication to save and restore America's democratic promise and make sure it continues to flourish for many years to come.

NOTE

Chapter 5: Technology and Democracy
  - Leveraging Social Media
  - Combating Misinformation

Chapter 5: Technology and Democracy
Leveraging Social Media: Amplifying Voices, Fostering Engagement

The world of democratic engagement has changed dramatically as a result of technology, especially social media platforms. This chapter examines the ways in which social media utilization can strengthen voices, promote civic involvement, and enable people to take an active role in political debate and decision-making processes.

Social Media's Ascent in Democracy

Social media sites like YouTube, Facebook, Twitter, Instagram, and others have made it easier for people to communicate and obtain information. They also allow people to interact with one another, exchange ideas, and rally support for political and social concerns. Politicians, advocacy organizations, and grassroots movements have never-before-seen chances to communicate with a wide range of people, spread their message, and interact with supporters in real time using these platforms.

Activating a Digital Viewership

Developing engaging material, interacting with followers, and utilizing digital analytics to comprehend audience preferences and behaviors are all essential components of an effective social media strategy. Online communities can be engaged, moved to action, and stimulated to take action by communicators using interactive elements, visual imagery, and storytelling tactics. Through social media campaigns, people may sign petitions, take part in virtual town halls, and plan events that will raise their voices and impact public opinion.

Strengthening Local Movements

Social media has given grassroots movements more capacity to enlist followers, spread the word about important topics, and promote social change on a local, national, and international level. Social media sites such as Twitter and Instagram enable the spread of viral campaigns that instantly reach millions of users, igniting discussions, building momentum, and inspiring group action towards common objectives. Social media has been essential in amplifying minority voices and igniting movements for social justice and political transformation, from the Arab Spring uprisings to the Black Lives Matter campaign.

Fighting False Information: Preserving Democratic Honesty

Social media provides chances for democratic participation, but it also has drawbacks, especially when it comes to battling online manipulation, misinformation, and disinformation. The methods for advancing media literacy, verifying information, and preserving democratic integrity in the digital era are discussed in this section.

Misinformation's Propagation

Misinformation is defined as incorrect or misleading information that accidentally spreads and is frequently the result of mistakes or misunderstandings. Disinformation, on the other hand, is the purposeful dissemination of false information with the aim to mislead, sway public opinion, or erode confidence in democratic institutions. Effectively addressing the difficulties of misinformation and disinformation propagation is crucial in order to safeguard electoral integrity, public discourse, and social cohesion.

Encouraging the Use of Media

The acquisition of media literacy skills is crucial in enabling users to assess information critically, differentiate dependable sources from untrustworthy ones, and recognize misleading strategies employed in digital content. By providing media literacy instruction in classrooms, community centers, and online, educators may enable people to properly manage the complexity of the digital world and take part in democratic decision-making with knowledge.

Verification of Facts and Accountability

By confirming statements, erasing errors, and holding those who spread false information responsible for their actions, fact-checking campaigns are essential in the fight against misinformation. News outlets, academic institutions, and independent fact-checkers work together to evaluate the veracity of material making the rounds online and to make their evaluations openly available to the general public. Promoting fact-based reporting and openness in media practices can help stakeholders lessen the negative effects of disinformation on democratic processes and public opinion.

Digital privacy and the ethical use of data

Maintaining integrity and confidence in democratic processes depends critically on ensuring the ethical use of data and safeguarding digital privacy. The significance of data ethics, privacy rights, and legal frameworks that protect people's private information and stop illegal access or misuse is discussed in this section.

Political Campaign Data Ethics

Advocacy groups and political campaigns frequently use data analytics and tailored advertising to target particular voter demographics with messages. Data-driven tactics can improve outreach and engagement, but they also bring up issues with consent, privacy rights, and the possibility of misusing or manipulating personal information. Respecting people's rights to privacy and autonomy as well as democratic principles depends on upholding ethical norms in the gathering, storing, and use of data.

Controlling Online Resources

When it comes to ethical issues like platform accountability, content control, and data protection, regulatory frameworks are essential. International organizations, governments, and legislators work together to create policies and guidelines that protect users from dangerous content and manipulative tactics, encourage openness in algorithmic decision-making, and regulate the behavior of digital platforms. Stakeholders can reduce risks related to online disinformation and protect democratic integrity by implementing laws that support democratic norms and create fair competition in the digital economy.

Utilizing Technology for Democratic Renewal in Conclusion

The revolutionary potential of technology in reviving democracy and enabling people to actively participate in civic life is highlighted in Chapter 5. Social media can be used by individuals to advocate for policy reforms, advance social justice, and hold elected officials responsible to their citizens by amplifying voices, fostering interaction, and mobilizing grassroots movements. However, tackling issues like disinformation and data privacy calls for coordinated efforts, media literacy initiatives, and laws that support democratic principles.

Let's responsibly use technology to promote democratic renewal and make sure that digital platforms act as catalysts for constructive social change as we traverse the potential and challenges of the digital age. People may contribute to a more inclusive, transparent, and resilient democracy—one that enables all citizens to actively engage in shaping a better future for our country—by learning how to effectively use technology through accessible means. By working together, we can preserve and restore America's democratic promise and make sure it continues to flourish for many years to come.

NOTE

Chapter 6: Policy and Reform
- Understanding Policy Impact
- Advocacy and Legislative Change

Chapter 5: Technology and Democracy
Leveraging Social Media: Amplifying Voices, Fostering Engagement

The world of democratic engagement has changed dramatically as a result of technology, especially social media platforms. This chapter examines the ways in which social media utilization can strengthen voices, promote civic involvement, and enable people to take an active role in political debate and decision-making processes.

Social Media's Ascent in Democracy

Social media sites like YouTube, Facebook, Twitter, Instagram, and others have made it easier for people to communicate and obtain information. They also allow people to interact with one another, exchange ideas, and rally support for political and social concerns. Politicians, advocacy organizations, and grassroots movements have never-before-seen chances to communicate with a wide range of people, spread their message, and interact with supporters in real time using these platforms.

Activating a Digital Viewership

Developing engaging material, interacting with followers, and utilizing digital analytics to comprehend audience preferences and behaviors are all essential components of an effective social media strategy. Online communities can be engaged, moved to action, and stimulated to take action by communicators using interactive elements, visual imagery, and storytelling tactics. Through social media campaigns, people may sign petitions, take part in virtual town halls, and plan events that will raise their voices and impact public opinion.

Strengthening Local Movements

Social media has given grassroots movements more capacity to enlist followers, spread the word about important topics, and promote social change on a local, national, and international level. Social media sites such as Twitter and Instagram enable the spread of viral campaigns that instantly reach millions of users, igniting discussions, building momentum, and inspiring group action towards common objectives. Social media has been essential in amplifying minority voices and igniting movements for social justice and political transformation, from the Arab Spring uprisings to the Black Lives Matter campaign.

Fighting False Information: Preserving Democratic Honesty

Social media provides chances for democratic participation, but it also has drawbacks, especially when it comes to battling online manipulation, misinformation, and disinformation. The methods for advancing media literacy, verifying information, and preserving democratic integrity in the digital era are discussed in this section.

Misinformation's Propagation

Misinformation is defined as incorrect or misleading information that accidentally spreads and is frequently the result of mistakes or misunderstandings. Disinformation, on the other hand, is the purposeful dissemination of false information with the aim to mislead, sway public opinion, or erode confidence in democratic institutions. Effectively addressing the difficulties of misinformation and disinformation propagation is crucial in order to safeguard electoral integrity, public discourse, and social cohesion.

Encouraging the Use of Media

The acquisition of media literacy skills is crucial in enabling users to assess information critically, differentiate dependable sources from untrustworthy ones, and recognize misleading strategies employed in digital content. By providing media literacy instruction in classrooms, community centers, and online, educators may enable people to properly manage the complexity of the digital world and take part in democratic decision-making with knowledge.

Verification of Facts and Accountability

By confirming statements, erasing errors, and holding those who spread false information responsible for their actions, fact-checking campaigns are essential in the fight against misinformation. News outlets, academic institutions, and independent fact-checkers work together to evaluate the veracity of material making the rounds online and to make their evaluations openly available to the general public. Promoting fact-based reporting and openness in media practices can help stakeholders lessen the negative effects of disinformation on democratic processes and public opinion.

Digital privacy and the ethical use of data

Maintaining integrity and confidence in democratic processes depends critically on ensuring the ethical use of data and safeguarding digital privacy. The significance of data ethics, privacy rights, and legal frameworks that protect people's private information and stop illegal access or misuse is discussed in this section.

Political Campaign Data Ethics

Advocacy groups and political campaigns frequently use data analytics and tailored advertising to target particular voter demographics with messages. Data-driven tactics can improve outreach and engagement, but they also bring up issues with consent, privacy rights, and the possibility of misusing or manipulating personal information. Respecting people's rights to privacy and autonomy as well as democratic principles depends on upholding ethical norms in the gathering, storing, and use of data.

Controlling Online Resources

When it comes to ethical issues like platform accountability, content control, and data protection, regulatory frameworks are essential. International organizations, governments, and legislators work together to create policies and guidelines that protect users from dangerous content and manipulative tactics, encourage openness in algorithmic decision-making, and regulate the behavior of digital platforms. Stakeholders can reduce risks related to online disinformation and protect democratic integrity by implementing laws that support democratic norms and create fair competition in the digital economy.

Utilizing Technology for Democratic Renewal in Conclusion

The revolutionary potential of technology in reviving democracy and enabling people to actively participate in civic life is highlighted in Chapter 5. Social media can be used by individuals to advocate for policy reforms, advance social justice, and hold elected officials responsible to their citizens by amplifying voices, fostering interaction, and mobilizing grassroots movements. However, tackling issues like disinformation and data privacy calls for coordinated efforts, media literacy initiatives, and laws that support democratic principles.

Let's responsibly use technology to promote democratic renewal and make sure that digital platforms act as catalysts for constructive social change as we traverse the potential and challenges of the digital age. People may contribute to a more inclusive, transparent, and resilient democracy—one that enables all citizens to actively engage in shaping a better future for our country—by learning how to effectively use technology through accessible means. By working together, we can preserve and restore America's democratic promise and make sure it continues to flourish for many years to come.

NOTE

Chapter 7: The Role of Youth in Democracy
  - Engaging the Next Generation
  - Empowering Young Voices

Chapter 7: Youth's Place in Democracy: Inspiring the Next Generation and Increasing Youth Involvement

Involving and empowering the upcoming generation of leaders and citizens is critical to the survival of democracy. This chapter examines how activism, advocacy, and creative approaches to social change can help young people revitalize democracy, promote civic engagement, and shape the political landscape.

Youth Activism's Power

Young people who engage in a variety of activities to promote social, political, and environmental causes that impact both their local communities and the global community are referred to as youth activists. Youth activists contribute new ideas, enthusiasm, and a feeling of urgency to urgent issues facing society today, ranging from gun control and climate action to racial justice movements and LGBTQ+ rights campaigns.

Strengthening Youth Voices

Giving young people the chance to voice their ideas, engage in decision-making processes, and contribute to policy discussions that affect their lives and futures is a key component of empowering young voices. Youth councils, student government associations, and youth-led groups that offer forums for advocacy training, skill development, and leadership development are just a few examples of the many ways that kids can be empowered.

Youth Engagement and Civic Education

In order to prepare young people to become knowledgeable and engaged citizens, civic education is essential. Through the provision of civics, political literacy, and critical thinking instruction at educational institutions and local communities, instructors can enable learners to comprehend their entitlements, accountabilities, and the significance of civic participation in molding a fairer and more impartial society.

Constructing Bridges Between Generations

Working together and having conversations across generations is crucial to mending gaps, promoting understanding, and utilizing the combined knowledge and experience of many age groups. This section looks at ways to foster collaborations, mentorship programs, and intergenerational cooperation between young activists and well-established figures in academia, politics, and civil society.

Development of Leadership and Mentoring

Through mentoring programs, young activists are paired with seasoned leaders who can offer them advice, encouragement, and support as they fulfill their duties as social change agents. Ensuring continuity in advocacy activities and leadership succession, these programs promote personal growth, skill development, and the transfer of information and skills across generations.

Innovation and Social Entrepreneurship Driven by Youth

Young people are given the tools they need to solve systemic injustices, come up with innovative solutions to societal problems, and bring about long-lasting change in their communities through youth-led innovation and social entrepreneurship. Youth can work together, develop ideas, and start projects that have a real influence on the local and global levels through platforms like hackathons, innovation laboratories, and incubator programs.

Youth Engagement and Digital Activism

Through online platforms and social media networks, digital technology has democratized access to knowledge and inspired youth to participate in action and advocacy. This section looks at how youth activism can be used to organize virtual campaigns, raise awareness of social justice issues, and mobilize support for legislative changes.

Using Social Media to Promote Causes

Youth activists can collect support for campaigns and protests, reach a wide audience, and bring attention to issues through social media platforms. Young people are empowered to share personal tales, interact with like-minded others, and create virtual communities centered around common values and goals through hashtag movements, viral challenges, and digital storytelling initiatives.

Possibilities and Difficulties of Digital Engagement

Although digital activism brings chances for adolescent empowerment and engagement, it also comes with drawbacks, such as the dissemination of false information, cyberbullying, and algorithmic biases that influence online interactions. Promoting responsible digital citizenship and defending democratic principles in the digital age need teaching young people about digital literacy, online safety, and ethical usage of digital platforms.

In conclusion, Developing the Next Wave of Leaders

The transforming power of youth involvement in reviving democracy and furthering social progress is highlighted in Chapter 7. A new generation of knowledgeable, compassionate, and resilient leaders who are dedicated to creating inclusive communities and upholding democratic ideals can be developed by individuals and groups through elevating the voices of the youth, encouraging civic education, and promoting intergenerational cooperation.

Let's offer opportunities for young people to contribute their skills, viewpoints, and creative ideas to the problems facing our planet as we harness the fervor and idealism of youth activism. We can guarantee that democracy stays dynamic, responsive, and inclusive by learning the best ways to empower and engage youngsters through approachable methods. This will allow all generations to actively participate in shaping a better future for our communities, our country, and the entire globe. By working together, we can preserve and restore America's democratic promise and make sure it continues to flourish for many years to come.

NOTE

Chapter 8: The Power of Unity
   - Building Alliances Across Divides
   - Collaborative Problem Solving

Chapter 8: The Power of Unity Building Alliances Across Divides: Strengthening Democratic Cohesion

Unity is the conscious development of a common goal and respect for one another rather than just the absence of division. To build inclusive spaces where varied voices are heard, valued, and empowered, it is necessary to bridge ideological, cultural, and socioeconomic divisions in the context of democracy in order to foster togetherness. This chapter examines how unity may advance democratic values, encourage group action, and address systemic issues that American society is currently confronting.

Recognizing Democracy's Divides

Diverse viewpoints and life experiences influence public debate and policy decisions, which is essential for democracy to flourish. On the other hand, entrenched differences in politics, society, or the economy can erode public confidence in institutions, exacerbate existing disparities, and impede the achievement of common objectives. Dialogue, empathy, and a dedication to discovering common ground that cuts over partisanship and ideological barriers are necessary to heal these divisions.

The Significance of Communication and Settlement

Dialogue is the first step in any effective unity-building strategy. These should be honest, open discussions that aim to comprehend opposing points of view, recognize historical injustices, and make amends for previous wrongs. Conversations increase empathy, trust, and a sense of shared accountability for resolving structural injustices and advancing social justice. Individuals and organizations can foster possibilities for healing, reconciliation, and solidarity across varied communities through facilitated discussions, community forums, and reconciliation programs.

Collaborative Issue Solving: Group Approaches to Communal Difficulties

Collaborative problem-solving is essential to democracy; individuals from different fields, specializations, and political affinities must come together to discover common problems and create inclusive solutions that benefit the entire community. The concepts of cooperative governance, coalition building, and cross-sector alliances are examined in this section in order to advance policy reforms and deal with urgent problems including healthcare access, economic inequality, and climate change.

Collaborative Governance Principles
The focus of collaborative governance is on inclusive decision-making procedures involving representatives of the public sector, private sector, civil society, and academic institutions. Collaborative governance is a means of promoting consensus-based approaches to difficult policy challenges and strengthening public trust in institutions by fostering transparency, accountability, and shared decision-making authority. Stakeholders can offer knowledge, materials, and a range of viewpoints to collaborative forums, task groups, and advisory councils in order to influence policy agendas and promote long-lasting change.

Building Advocacy Alliances and Coalitions

Coalition building is the process of bringing together various stakeholders, such as labor unions, faith-based communities, grassroots organizations, and advocacy groups, to promote policy changes and raise the voices of the group on matters of shared interest. Coalitions offer a forum for organizing grassroots support, coordinating advocacy initiatives, and gaining combined sway over local, state, and federal decision-makers. Through the formation of strategic alliances, stakeholders can take advantage of pools of resources, knowledge, and networks in order to bring about systemic change and advance fair results for underserved populations.

Increasing Social Cohesion by Developing Resilience and Trust

Social cohesion, or the links of reciprocity, trust, and support that unite people and communities, is strengthened by unity. In order to alleviate systemic inequality, develop inclusive communities where everyone may prosper and participate to democratic renewal, and promote social cohesion, strategies for doing so are examined in this section.

Encouragement of Inclusive Practices and Policies

All people, regardless of color, ethnicity, gender, or socioeconomic background, are guaranteed fair access to opportunities, resources, and services that improve their quality of life and general well-being through inclusive policies and practices. Policymakers can remove obstacles to social mobility and advance a more equitable and inclusive society by supporting anti-discrimination legislation, affirmative action initiatives, and inclusive economic development plans.

Increasing Conviction in Democratic Organizations

For governing systems to be legitimate and effective, trust in democratic institutions is necessary. The establishment and sustenance of public trust in government is contingent upon the principles of transparency, accountability, and responsiveness to citizen concerns. Elected politicians and other public workers may build civic engagement, trust, and democratic resilience during difficult times by embracing moral norms, respecting democratic ideals, and having meaningful conversations with their constituents.

In conclusion, promoting democracy via cooperation and unity

The transforming effect of unity in reviving democracy and encouraging group action to address structural issues is emphasized in Chapter 8. A more inclusive, resilient, and egalitarian society where all perspectives are heard and respected can be built by individuals and groups through bridging gaps, encouraging cooperative problem-solving, and advancing social cohesion. In order to preserve and resurrect America's democratic potential, readers are urged by this chapter to adopt the values of solidarity, cooperation, and togetherness.

Let's use unity to create common ground, encourage shared prosperity, and further the common good as we negotiate the challenges of democratic governance. People can contribute to a more cohesive, compassionate, and responsive democracy—one that values diversity, upholds justice, and enables all citizens to fully engage in forming a better future for our country and the world—by learning the most effective strategies for forming alliances across divides through approachable channels. By working together, we can make sure that America's democratic values are upheld for many years to come.

NOTE

Chapter 9: Sustainable Civic Engagement - Long-term Strategies - Creating a Culture of Participation

Chapter 9: Sustainable Civic Engagement
Long-term Strategies: Ensuring Enduring Participation

In order to be sustainable, civic engagement must be woven into society as a continuous, robust culture of participation rather than being limited to sporadic or episodic agitation. This chapter explores long-term tactics that can guarantee sustained civic engagement by looking at the systems and customs that maintain democratic engagement between generations.

Putting Civic Education Into Institutions

Comprehensive and continuous civic education is one of the cornerstones of long-term civic engagement. People should be raised with the ideals, information, and abilities needed to engage in democratic processes from an early age until maturity. In order to provide civic education that covers the background of democracy, the operation of political institutions, and the significance of active citizenship, schools, universities, and community organizations are essential.

Ongoing Education and Training

Civic education ought to be a lifetime endeavor, not just something that happens in the classroom. Citizens can stay educated about current topics, policy debates, and new forms of civic engagement through online courses, workshops, and continuous learning initiatives. Hubs for continuing civic education can be found in public libraries, community centers, and online resources, which will help to create an informed and involved populace.

Institutional Encouragement of Public Engagement

Structures and rewards that promote ongoing civic engagement can be established by governments and civic associations. To guarantee that citizens are always heard in decision-making, it is possible to institutionalize channels for public input by establishing citizen assemblies, advisory councils, and participatory budgeting procedures. Regular interaction opportunities offered by these institutions can facilitate individuals' long-term involvement.

Establishing a Participatory Culture: Promoting Democratic Principles and Norms

Democratic norms and values that place a high priority on mutual respect, active citizenship, and collective responsibility serve as the foundation of a long-lasting culture of participation. How to cultivate such a culture in communities and society at large is covered in this section.

Encouraging Civic Principles

Establishing civic virtues like accountability, compassion, and unity is crucial to developing a culture of engagement. Civic ideals can be incorporated into public discourse, community programs, and school curricula to emphasize the value of group problem-solving and active participation. Celebrating civic holidays, honoring public servants, and showcasing effective instances of civic engagement can encourage and inspire people to work toward the common good.

Social Capital and Community Development

The foundation of long-term civic involvement is made up of robust, connected communities. Communities can become more resilient and capable of taking collective action when they establish social capital networks of relationships, trust, and reciprocity. People are more willing to participate in civic affairs and help one another out when they are in need when social ties are strengthened and a sense of belonging is fostered through neighborhood associations, local events, and community-building activities.

Fair and Inclusive Participation

Maintaining civic participation requires making sure that everyone in society has an equal opportunity to engage. Incorporating underrepresented and underprivileged groups into civic activities can improve the diversity and depth of democratic participation. In order to create an inclusive civic culture where everyone can offer their thoughts and talents, it is imperative to remove barriers to participation, such as language challenges, accessibility issues, and socioeconomic restraints.

Activating Diverse Groups: Leveraging Pluralism's Power

Diverse populations enhance democratic dialogue and decision-making by bringing a multitude of experiences, viewpoints, and ideas to the table. The methods for involving a variety of demographics in long-term civic involvement are examined in this section.

Cultural Acuity and Perceptiveness

To effectively engage various communities, civic organizations and institutions need to cultivate cultural competence and sensitivity. This entails being aware of and respectful of other cultural norms, beliefs, and communication styles as well as establishing inclusive environments where everyone is made to feel important and welcome. Multicultural activities, diversity initiatives, and training programs can build mutual respect and improve cultural competency across varied communities.

Youth Engagement Across Generations

Maintaining civic engagement across generations requires involving youth and encouraging intergenerational cooperation. Through youth councils, mentorship programs, and intergenerational conversations, gaps in generations can be closed and young people can gain knowledge from seasoned leaders while also contributing new ideas and viewpoints to civic engagement. Encouraging youngsters and fostering intergenerational collaborations helps guarantee that civic engagement stays innovative and forward-thinking.

Using Technology to Promote Engagement Over Time

Technology provides platforms for ongoing communication, information exchange, and group action, making it one of the most effective tools for maintaining civic engagement. The use of technology to improve sustained civic engagement is examined in this section.

Digital Resources for Public Participation

Digital platforms that make it easy and accessible for people to interact, communicate, and take action—such as social media, online forums, and mobile apps—can support continued civic engagement. These platforms allow for ongoing participation across geographic boundaries by hosting virtual town halls, citizen feedback portals, and advocacy campaigns.

Data-Informed Engagement Techniques

Governments and civic organizations can use data analytics to better understand participation trends, spot gaps, and develop plans to increase involvement. Through the examination of voter turnout, community involvement, and social media interactions, stakeholders may create focused outreach programs, enhance their engagement endeavors, and track the success of their projects over an extended period of time.

Building a Robust Democratic Future in Conclusion

The necessity of sustained civic engagement is emphasized in Chapter 9 as a means of reviving democracy and guaranteeing its viability for future generations. A strong foundation for ongoing democratic renewal can be established by individuals and groups through the use of long-term tactics, the promotion of a culture of participation, the engagement of various populations, and the use of technology.

Let's commit to creating a robust democratic future where every voice is heard, every person is respected, and every community prospers as we work to understand the best methods to maintain civic involvement through approachable means. We can make sure that democracy is alive, inclusive, and sensitive to the interests and goals of every member of society by fostering a culture of active citizenry. By working together, we can restore and revive America's democratic promise and make sure it continues to thrive for many years to come.

NOTE

Chapter 10: Success Stories

- Case Studies of Democracy in Action
- Lessons Learned from Effective Movements

Chapter 10: Success Stories Case Studies of Democracy in Action: Real-World Examples of Democratic Renewal

The ability of a democracy to change, adapt, and meet the needs of its citizens is what makes it fundamental. Numerous success examples demonstrate how people, communities, and movements have successfully revived democratic systems and brought about significant change both domestically and internationally. In-depth case studies of democracy in action are provided in this chapter, highlighting creative solutions, community-based projects, and legislative changes that have improved democratic participation and governance.

1. Civil Rights Movement: A History of Equity and Fairness

In the history of American democracy, the Civil Rights Movement of the 1950s and 1960s is seen as a tremendous success story. Millions of people were inspired by the movement, which was led by figures like John Lewis, Rosa Parks, and Martin Luther King Jr., to use civil disobedience, peaceful protest, and legal challenges to fight for racial equality and eliminate segregation. By eliminating institutionalized racism and extending civil liberties, significant accomplishments like the Voting Rights Act of 1965 and the Civil Rights Act of 1964 revolutionized American culture.

Lessons Learned: - Grassroots Mobilization's Power: The movement showed how effective grassroots organizing can be in bringing about change and confronting structural injustice.

- The Significance of Nonviolent Protest: This method of protest has been successful in winning over the people and gaining support from other countries.
- Leadership and Unity: Maintaining momentum and winning legislation required charismatic leaders and a unified front.

2. New York City's Participatory Budgeting: Using Direct Democracy to Empower Citizens

A novel political mechanism called participatory budgeting (PB) gives citizens the power to choose how to divide up public monies. When PB was first implemented in New York City in 2011, it involved thousands of people in deliberative decision-making, which promoted accountability, openness, and community empowerment. PB has increased civic engagement, bolstered community ties, and made sure that public spending matches the needs and priorities of various communities by including locals in the budgeting process for local projects.

Lessons Learned: - Improving Accountability and Transparency: PB holds public servants responsible to community preferences and promotes transparency in government.
- Building Community Trust: Active participation in budgeting increases civic engagement by fostering trust between the public and the government.
- Inclusive Decision-Making: By guaranteeing the participation of marginalized and underrepresented groups in public spending, PB fosters inclusion and equity.

3. The Marriage Equality Movement: Securing LGBTQ+ Rights' Legal Recognition
The 2015 Obergefell v. Hodges ruling from the Supreme Court was a significant success in the fight for marriage equality in the United States by allowing same-sex unions to be legally recognized across the country.

Decades of lobbying, calculated legal action, public awareness campaigns, and grassroots mobilization by LGBTQ+ activists and supporters led to this victory. The campaign promoted greater societal acceptance of LGBTQ+ people in addition to securing legal recognition for same-sex couples.

Lessons Learned: - Strategic Litigation: Securing judicial recognition of marital equality and promoting civil rights required legal battles.
- Effective Messaging: Campaigns for public education that focused on family values, love, and commitment connected with a larger audience and increased support for marriage equality.
- Coalition Building: By forming partnerships with other groups and communities, the movement was able to spread its influence and encourage unity.

4. Flint, Michigan Environmental Justice: Community-Based Clean Water Advocacy

Public health and environmental justice issues received national attention as a result of the Flint, Michigan, water crisis. Local activists, community leaders, and groups such as the Flint Water Coalition united to demand safe drinking water and hold politicians responsible when the health of people was jeopardized by lead-contaminated water. Because of their advocacy, the situation was addressed and further suffering was averted through important legislative adjustments, infrastructural upgrades, and court settlements.

Lessons Learned: - Community lobbying: Affected people' tenacious lobbying played a critical role in drawing attention to the situation and applying pressure on the authorities to act.
- Intersectionality: The crisis brought attention to the ways that economic, racial, and environmental inequalities overlap, highlighting the necessity for all-encompassing remedies.
- Policy and Accountability: To ensure justice and long-term public health protections, legal action and policy reforms were crucial.

Crucial Lessons for Democratic Renewal from Successful Movements

The success stories in this chapter provide insightful information about the ideas and methods that underpin successful democratic renewal. We may draw important lessons from the tactics, difficulties, and results of these campaigns that will guide our future attempts to advance civic engagement and democracy.

1. The Influence of Local Organizing

A strong tool for bringing about democratic change is grassroots organizing. Driving systemic reform requires organizing people locally, encouraging community involvement, and creating support networks. Grassroots movements ensure that democratic procedures reflect the desire of the people by utilizing the combined power of common folks.

2. Why Strategic Advocacy Is Important

Clear objectives, focused efforts, and strategic planning are necessary for effective advocacy. A variety of advocacy strategies are used by successful movements, such as media campaigns, public protests, legal challenges, and lobbying activities. Combining these tactics allows activists to influence public opinion, put pressure on policymakers, and produce real policy results.

3. Inclusive Participation's Function

Ensuring egalitarian and representative democratic processes necessitates inclusive participation. Building a more inclusive democracy requires involving underrepresented and marginalized people, removing obstacles to participation, and promoting broad alliances. In addition to enhancing democratic legitimacy, inclusive involvement adds a greater range of viewpoints and experiences to decision-making.

4. The Need for Continual and Flexible Work

Restoring democracy demands tenacity and flexibility. Resilient movements are able to overcome obstacles and adjust to shifting conditions. Robust organizational frameworks, long-term financing sources, and the capacity to galvanize and maintain public support are the cornerstones of this resilience.

5. The Significance of Skillful Leadership

In order to direct democratic movements and motivate group action, leadership is essential. Proficient leaders has vision, charm, and the ability to rally support from many groups. They ensure that movements stay coherent and focused by fostering unity, establishing trust, and offering strategic direction.

Inspiring Next Generations of Democratic Activists: A Conclusion

In Chapter 10, the victories of democratic renewal are celebrated, and the significance of drawing lessons from the past to motivate present and future endeavors is emphasized. This chapter offers a road map for people and organizations dedicated to enhancing democratic engagement and governance by looking at case studies of democracy in action and highlighting important lessons.

As we take inspiration from these success stories, let us acknowledge the value of inclusive participation, the strength of group effort, and the significance of strategic advocacy. America's democratic values can continue to thrive for future generations if we learn how to effectively foster and maintain democratic renewal through practical measures.

By working together, we can create a dynamic, welcoming, and strong democracy that represents the objectives and ambitions of all of its people. Through historical analysis and the adoption of successful movement ideals, we can design a course for the future that respects our democratic heritage and leads to a more promising and just society.

NOTE

Conclusion: A Path Forward

- Recap of Key Strategies
- The Future of American Democracy

A Path Forward
Recap of Key Strategies

Upon finishing "Democracy Revival: Mastering the Best Ways to Rescue America Through Easy Means," it is imperative that we take a moment to consider the journey that the previous chapters have brought us on. We have looked at the various issues that American democracy is currently facing, as well as creative and doable methods for reviving civic involvement and real-world success stories that can serve as an example and source of inspiration. Now let us review the main approaches that came out of our investigation, emphasizing their importance and the ways in which they work together to support a strong democratic renewal.

1. Being Aware of the Obstacles

We started out by being aware of the significant obstacles that modern American democracy faces. These issues, which range from voter suppression and the role of money in politics to political polarization and the decline in public trust in institutions, pose a danger to the fundamental basis of democratic administration. Acknowledging these problems is the first step toward solving them since it enables us to create focused plans and organize group initiatives to go over them.

2. Giving Each Person Power

Individual empowerment is the cornerstone of the democratic comeback. Since informed citizens are better able to engage effectively in democratic processes, civic education and awareness are vital. A strong emphasis on voting rights, the promotion of informed decision-making, and the cultivation of a feeling of civic responsibility are necessary to guarantee that people actively participate in the democratic fabric of society.

3. Creating Community Links

Communities that are robust and cohesive are essential to the survival of democracy. Local groups and grassroots movements are essential for promoting social capital development, encouraging civic engagement, and tackling concerns unique to a community. We can build a solid basis for democratic engagement by fostering cooperative problem-solving and fostering stronger community links.

4. Politics: The Art of Effective Communication

Overcoming polarization and promoting productive debate require bridging gaps and having civil conversations. In order to communicate effectively in politics, one must be empathetic, actively listen, and dedicated to discovering common ground. We can improve democratic discussion and decision-making by placing a high value on polite conversation and cultivating a respectful society.

5. Using Technology to Promote Democracy

Technology provides effective methods to improve democratic participation. Digital platforms, social media, and data analytics can all help to promote ongoing communication, information exchange, and group action. However, maximizing the benefits of technology while reducing its perils requires battling false information and guaranteeing digital literacy.

6. Reform and Policy

In order to solve systemic challenges, it is imperative that advocates for legislative reform understand the impact of policies. Strategic preparation, coalition building, and persistent efforts to sway officials are all necessary for effective advocacy. We can establish a democratic system that is more responsive and just by advocating for policies that improve accountability, transparency, and equity.

7. Involving Young People

One cannot emphasize the importance of young in democracies. It is possible to guarantee that the opinions of the younger generation are acknowledged and heard by involving them in education, mentoring, and empowerment programs. We can develop a vibrant and progressive democratic culture by encouraging intergenerational cooperation and giving young people leadership opportunities.

8. The Strength of Cooperation

A strong force for democratic renewal is unity. To tackle complicated difficulties, it is imperative to establish cooperative problem-solving, solidarity, and partnerships across differences. We can build a society that is more inclusive and cohesive by placing a higher priority on unity and group efforts.

9. Long-Term Civic Participation

A participation-oriented culture and long-term plans are necessary for sustainable civic engagement. Ensuring sustained democratic participation requires institutionalizing civic education, encouraging lifelong learning, and offering institutional support for civic engagement. We may forge inclusive and equitable engagement opportunities and therefore construct a robust democratic future.

10. Taking A Hint from Success Stories

Democratic renewal success stories provide insightful information and motivation. By looking at case studies of successful movements and extracting important lessons, we can make future attempts to fortify democracy more informed. The possibility for significant change is emphasized by recurrent themes such as the effectiveness of inclusive participation, strategic lobbying, grassroots organizing strength, and successful leadership.

The Prospects for American Democracy

Future prospects for American democracy both bright and difficult at the same time. The tactics and ideas we have studied in this book offer a thorough road map for reviving democratic participation and government. Nonetheless, achieving a more dynamic, inclusive, and resilient democracy calls for teamwork, unwavering dedication, and a clear understanding of what is best for everyone.

1. Accepting Accountability

The desire of each person to accept civic duty will determine the fate of American democracy. More than just casting a ballot, active citizenship also entails keeping up with current events, engaging in public conversation, fighting for justice, and improving the welfare of one's community. We can guarantee that democracy continues to be vibrant and adaptable by encouraging a culture of civic duty.

2. Promoting Equity and Inclusivity

Prioritizing equity and inclusivity is crucial if we are to improve democracy. A genuinely representative and just democratic system can only be established by guaranteeing that all views are heard, eliminating obstacles to participation, and tackling underlying imbalances. Prioritizing fairness and inclusivity will help us create a society that is stronger and more unified.

3. Fostering Accountability and Transparency

Democratic government is based on the principles of accountability and transparency. To keep the public's trust and avoid corruption, public institutions must be run with transparency and honesty. We can strengthen democratic accountability by supporting investigative journalism, pushing for transparency laws, and holding public officials responsible.

4. Promoting Civil Conversation

Finding common ground and overcoming political disagreements require civil discourse. Encouraging polite conversation, attentive listening, and empathy can aid in bridging gaps and encouraging positive involvement. We can foster a more cooperative and peaceful political atmosphere by promoting polite conversation.

5. Leveraging Technology's Potential

The future of democracy will be significantly shaped by technology for some time to come. To fully realize the promise of technology, we must address the issues of misinformation and data privacy, encourage digital literacy, and use digital tools for civic engagement. We can improve democracy and governance by embracing innovation while defending democratic principles.

6. Encouragement of Youth Leadership

The next generation will determine the course of democracy. In order to make sure that young people are equipped to lead and contribute to democratic renewal, it is imperative that we support youth leadership, offer opportunities for civic education, and encourage intergenerational collaboration. We can guarantee a dynamic and progressive democratic future by empowering the youth.

7. Establishing Sturdy Organizations

Democratic institutions must be resilient in order to endure setbacks and adjust to changing circumstances. To ensure that democratic institutions can successfully serve the public interest, it is essential to promote strong checks and balances, preserve the integrity of election processes, and strengthen the independence of the judiciary.

8. Fostering Optimism and Hope

Lastly, maintaining the momentum of democratic regeneration requires fostering optimism and hope. While democracy has many obstacles, there is also a great deal of opportunity for improvement. By recognizing accomplishments, appreciating advancements, and keeping an optimistic attitude, we may encourage ongoing efforts to fortify democracy.

An Appeal for Intervention

To sum up, "Democracy Revival: Mastering the Best Ways to Rescue America Through Easy Means" serves as a roadmap for negotiating the challenges of democratic regeneration in addition to being a call to action. A thorough framework for tackling the problems facing American democracy and promoting a more dynamic, inclusive, and resilient democratic future is offered by the tactics and ideas presented in this book.

As we go, let's make a commitment to upholding civic duty, encouraging diversity and equity, encouraging openness and accountability, encouraging polite conversation, utilizing technology to its fullest, assisting young people in leadership roles, creating strong institutions, and encouraging hope and optimism. We can make sure that America's democratic ideals survive and thrive for many decades to come by cooperating and taking inspiration from the successful stories of democratic renewal.

It is up to us to decide how American democracy will evolve. Let's step up to the plate, learn how to save and reinvigorate our democracy, and open the door for a more promising, just, and equal future for all. By working together, we can create a democracy that genuinely represents the potential, goals, and aspirations of each and every person as well as community.

NOTE

APPENDIX

Appendix: Civic Engagement Resources

Access to resources is critical to our efforts to restore democracy and promote an active participation culture. An extensive list of resources—including organizations, programs, and tools—that can assist people and communities in participating in the democratic process more successfully is included in this appendix section. These materials will enable you to take effective action and support democratic renewal, regardless of your experience level as an activist or your level of civic engagement.

1. Registration and Information for Voters

A fundamental aspect of democratic participation is guaranteeing that each and every eligible citizen is registered to vote and knowledgeable about the political process. Information about voter registration, voting rights, and election procedures can be found in the following resources:

- Vote.org: A nonpartisan website that provides resources for polling place searching, absentee ballot requests, and voter registration.
- An organization called Rock the Vote works to get young people involved in politics by offering resources for voter registration, election reminders, and voting rights education.
- When We All Vote: A nonpartisan, nationwide campaign that offers resources for voter registration and civic education aimed at increasing voter turnout.

2. Awareness and Education for Civic Engagement

Developing informed citizens requires civic education. These resources provide instructional materials, programs, and courses to improve civic awareness and knowledge:
- iCivics: Judge Sandra Day O'Connor founded this website, which offers free instructional games and lesson plans to teach civics to kids and promote

 involvement.
- The Civics Renewal Network: An alliance of institutions offering free, excellent resources for teaching civics to teachers and students.
- Center for Civic Education: This group offers curricula and teacher professional development in an effort to advance civic education in schools.

3. Lobbying and Changing Policies

Advocacy groups are essential for influencing legislation and promoting social change. The following organizations provide resources, instruction, and assistance to people and communities promoting legislative change:

- The American Civil Liberties Union (ACLU): A nonprofit that provides tools for advocacy and legal action while defending and upholding individual rights and liberties.
Common Cause is a grassroots, nonpartisan group that provides advocacy and policy reform tools while working to preserve the fundamental principles of American democracy.
- Indivisible: A network of neighborhood organizations that promotes progressive change and offers tools for policy lobbying and grassroots organizing.

4. Local and grassroots movements and organizing

Building local authority and tackling concerns unique to a community need community organizing. These tools aid community-based groups and grassroots movements:

- Community Tool Box: An extensive online resource that provides helpful advice for advocacy, program development, and community organization.
- The Center for Community Change: This group uses advocacy and organizing to enable low-income individuals to improve their neighborhoods.
- PICO National Network: This network of faith-based community

organizers seeks to develop creative answers to urgent regional and national problems.

5. Digital Resources for Public Participation
By offering venues for information sharing, mobilization, and communication, technology can improve civic engagement. The following digital resources encourage advocacy and civic engagement:

- Change.org: A website that enables users to start and sign petitions on a variety of topics, rallying support and influencing policymakers.
Countable: An app that simplifies the process of understanding and adhering to laws, corresponding with elected officials, and taking part in advocacy efforts.
- Next door: A neighborhood-focused social networking site that promotes information sharing, neighborhood organizing, and local communication.

6. Grants & Funding for Community Initiatives

Funding is often a problem for community projects. These resources offer details on grants and financing opportunities for groups and civic projects:

- The Fund for Democratic Communities: Offers funding and assistance to initiatives that improve civic participation and democracy.
- The Open Society Foundations: Provides support for projects that advance human rights, democracy, and justice.
The Kellogg Foundation: Provides funding for initiatives that strengthen the lives of disadvantaged children and families, emphasizing civic and community involvement.

7. Public Service and Volunteering

One effective strategy to support community well-being and democratic renewal is through volunteering. The following groups provide chances for community involvement and volunteer work:

- AmeriCorps: A national service initiative that gives citizens of the United States the chance to serve their communities and the public good. Volunteer Match is an internet resource that links volunteers with community projects and charitable organizations.
- DoSomething.org: A website that uses campaigns and volunteer opportunities to get young people involved in social action.

Suggested Reading

The following books and articles offer insightful analysis, relevant background, and helpful advice for anybody looking to expand their knowledge of democracy, civic involvement, and social change. This list of suggested readings covers a wide range of subjects and includes viewpoints from academics, activists, and influential people.

Books about Civic Engagement and Democracy

1. Alexis de Tocqueville, "Democracy in America": - A timeless text that offers insights into the nature of democratic administration while analyzing the advantages and disadvantages of American democracy in the early 19th century.

2. "The Federalist Papers" authored by John Jay, James Madison, and Alexander Hamilton: - An assortment of compositions promoting the adoption of the United States Constitution, delving into the fundamentals of democratic governance and the significance of checks and balances.

3. Robert D. Putnam's "Bowling Alone: The Collapse and Revival of American Community": - A landmark study that examines how America's social capital is eroding and how it affects democratic participation, along with recommendations for reviving community involvement.

4. Robert D. Putnam's "Our Kids: The American Dream in Crisis": - An examination of the nation's rising inequality and how it affects democracy, emphasizing the value of social mobility and equitable opportunity.

5. "How Democracies Die" by Steven Levitsky and Daniel Ziblatt: - A critique of the indicators and processes via which democracies might implode, based on both historical and modern case studies.

6. Grace Lee Boggs' book "The Next American Revolution: Sustainable Activism for the Twenty-First Century":
   - An innovative study that emphasizes the significance of community-based transformation and asks for a fundamental rethinking of activism and democracy in light of current issues.

Activism and Civic Education Books

1. Elizabeth Kaufer Busch and Jonathan W. White's "Civic Education and the Future of American Citizenship": a thorough analysis of the situation of civic education in the United States and its vital role in producing knowledgeable and involved citizens.

2. James Youniss and Peter Levine, editors, "Engaging Young People in Civic Life":
   - a compilation of writings that examine the value of young people participating in civic life and tactics for enabling the upcoming democratic generation.

3. Saul Alinsky's book "Rules for Radicals: A Practical Primer for Realistic Radicals":
   - A famous manual on grassroots activism and community organizing that provides helpful guidance on bringing about social change.

4. Andrew Boyd, editor, "Beautiful Trouble: A Toolbox for Revolution":
  - A creatively organized collection of case studies, techniques, and ideas for creative activism, geared for individuals trying to change their communities and beyond.

Articles and Reports on Democracy and Civic Participation 1. John Dewey's "Democracy and Education": - A well-known article that highlights the importance of education in promoting engaged citizenry and makes the case for the inclusion of democratic values in the curriculum.

2. Aaron Smith's "Civic Engagement in the Digital Age": - an investigation into how digital technologies affect political and civic engagement, published by the Pew Research Center.

3. The National Endowment for Democracy's "The Role of Civil Society in Democracy" examines the vital roles that civil society organizations play in advancing civic engagement and assisting democratic governance.

4. The Democracy Fund's "The State of American Democracy: How to Revive Our Democratic Culture": - an extensive analysis that evaluates American democracy now and makes suggestions for reviving civic participation.

5. Peter Levine's paper "Youth Civic Engagement: An Institutional Turn" delves into the significance of institutional backing for youth civic engagement and offers tactics for cultivating a culture of participation among the youth.

Concluding Remarks: Enduring Readers to Promote Democratic Rebirth

For those looking to get more involved in democracy and help bring it back, this appendix is a great resource. Through granting individuals and communities access to an abundance of resources, associations, and instructional materials, our aim is to enable them to take significant action and effect positive change.

Readers are encouraged to delve further into the complex fabric of democratic theory and practice by the wide range of viewpoints and ideas included in the suggested reading list. By interacting with these texts, readers can deepen their comprehension of democratic ideals, hone their civic engagement abilities, and find motivation in the struggles and triumphs of the past.

As we come to the end of "Democracy Revival: Mastering the Best Ways to Rescue America Through Easy Means," let us keep in mind the lessons discovered, the approaches presented, and the motivation acquired. By working together, we can create a democracy that is more robust, inclusive, and dynamic and that represents the goals and aspirations of all of its people.

ACKNOWLEDEGEMENTS

ACKNOWLEDGEMENTS
Writing "Democracy Revival: Mastering the Best Ways to Rescue America Through Easy Means" has been an incredible adventure made possible by the help, advice, and contributions of many outstanding people and organizations. This book is as much theirs as it is mine, and I appreciate their vital contributions in its making with deep gratitude and admiration.

Thank You to All the Donors and Advocates

1. Scholars and Thought Leaders

Above all, I owe a profound debt of appreciation to the academics and thought leaders whose ground-breaking work served as the inspiration for this book. Their studies, publications, and lectures have shed light on the nuances of civic participation and democracy, providing insights that have influenced my perspective and methodology.

- Dr. Robert D. Putnam, whose groundbreaking books "Our Kids" and "Bowling Alone" had a significant impact on how I thought about social capital, community involvement, and the value of creating robust, cohesive communities.
- Drs. Daniel Ziblatt and Steven Levitsky, whose research in "How Democracies Die" has been crucial in helping us comprehend the weaknesses and adaptability of democratic systems.
- Grace Lee Boggs, whose forward-thinking concepts in "The Next American Revolution" prompted a reconsideration of activism and the significance of neighborhood-based reform in democratic rebirth.

2. Civic Activists and Teachers

The cultivation of an informed and involved citizenry has been greatly aided by the efforts of civic educators and campaigners. Their commitment to encouraging civic engagement and knowledge has been a source of inspiration and hope.

- The staff at iCivics, which Justice Sandra Day O'Connor founded, for their steadfast dedication to offering top-notch resources for civic education that enable youth to become engaged, informed citizens.
- The Common Cause, for their unwavering advocacy in upholding the fundamental principles of American democracy and their support in providing tools for grassroots organizing and policy reform; and The Center for Civic Education, whose efforts to advance civic education in schools have been crucial in molding the next generation of democratic participants.

3. Community Organizers and Ground-Up Movements

The backbone of democratic participation are grassroots movements and community organizers, who put up endless effort to tackle regional problems and bring about constructive change from the bottom up. Throughout this effort, their bravery, tenacity, and dedication have served as an inspiration.

- The Indivisible organizers and volunteers, whose grass-roots campaigns to demand progressive change and hold elected officials responsible have shown the effectiveness of group action.
- The PICO National Network's faith-based community organizers, for their dedication to using community organizing to develop creative solutions to urgent local and national concerns. The Center for Community Change has played a pivotal role in promoting social justice and democratic renewal by enabling low-income communities to effect positive change.

4. Digital Pioneers and Activists

Technology has developed into a potent weapon for activism and civic involvement in the digital era. By utilizing these tools, activists and inventors have significantly democratized knowledge and galvanized support for worthy causes.

- The Change.org team, for offering an easily navigable petition creation and signing platform that enables people to rally support and sway policymakers on a variety of causes.
- The folks behind Countable, an app that has simplified the process of understanding and adhering to laws, contacting elected officials, and taking part in advocacy campaigns for users.
- The neighborhood at Next door, which uses its social networking site to promote neighborhood organizing and local communication, enabling neighbors to get together and work together on civic projects.

5. Funding Agencies and Philanthropists

Civic initiatives frequently struggle to secure finance, and the kindness of benefactors and funding organizations has been essential in sustaining the efforts of innumerable people and organizations committed to democratic renewal.

- The Fund for Democratic Communities, for funding initiatives aimed at enhancing civic participation and democracy.
- The Open Society Foundations, for their continuous financial support and promotion of justice, democratic governance, and human rights.
- The Kellogg Foundation, for its commitment to enhancing living circumstances for underprivileged kids and families, with an emphasis on civic and community involvement.

Individual Recognitions

1. Friends and Family
One of the most important aspects of this trip has been my family's and friends' constant support. Their support, empathy, and conviction in the value of this work have helped me get through the difficulties and successes of producing this book.

- To my spouse, whose tolerance, affection, and unwavering support have served as my pillars. Your confidence in me and this endeavor has given me a great deal of strength and inspiration.
- Thank you to my kids for helping me understand how important the future we are creating is. Your inquisitiveness, queries, and observations have motivated and anchored me.
- To my friends, whose understanding and support have been priceless. It has meant the world to me that you are willing to listen, provide criticism, and experience the highs and lows of this trip with me.

2. Advisors and Mentors

This work has benefited greatly from the advice and insight of my mentors and advisors. Their advice, encouragement, and criticism has helped me hone my concepts and finish this project.

- Dr. Abel, I appreciate your rigorous thinking and considerate criticism, which have forced me to consider the problems at hand in a more profound and critical manner.
- Mr. Manuel, for your wise counsel and tactical direction, which have been invaluable in helping me work through this project's challenge
for your wise advice and cooperative nature, which have greatly enhanced this job.

3. Those who read and encourage

Lastly, I would want to express my sincere gratitude to all of the supporters and readers of "Democracy Revival: Mastering the Best Ways to Rescue America Through Easy Means." Your participation, suggestions, and commitment to democratic values are what motivated the writing of this book. My goal is that this effort will motivate you to get engaged, take initiative, and support the rebirth of our democracy.

In summary

Upon contemplating the process of writing this book, I am overwhelmed with appreciation for all the people and institutions who helped make it possible. This initiative has been a team effort, enabled by the inspiration, leadership, and support of many individuals committed to the cause of democratic renewal.

I sincerely thank each and every one of you. Your dedication to building a more dynamic, inclusive, and resilient democracy is evidence of the long-lasting influence of civic involvement and group effort. We can create a future that represents the objectives and aspirations of all of its people if we work together.

I appreciate you traveling with me on this trip. Let's keep cooperating to figure out how to preserve and bolster our democracy so that it can serve as a source of opportunity and hope for future generations.

9 798329 938890